# Through the dark, we'll be alright

Harriett Smith

BookLeaf Publishing

India | USA | UK

Presentation by *BookLeaf Publishing*

Web: www.bookleafpub.com

E-mail: info@bookleafpub.com


ISBN: 9789357446419

First edition 2022

# DEDICATION

for Rosa; my life, my recovery and my future.

# ACKNOWLEDGE MENT

Thanks to my mum and dad for supporting and encouraging me. Thank you to my brother Michael; you are my best friend and I wouldn't still be here without you. Mum, dad and Michael; I am so grateful for all the time, love and patience you have shown me over the last 6 years; thank you for the cards, all the hospital visits, the phone calls of me crying that lasted for hours, the texts that you sent me constantly and for truly believing in me.

Thank you to the staff at Woodbourne Priory hospital in Birmingham; thank you for the endless support and encouragement, all the games of bananagrams, for wiping away my tears and holding me while I cried, for never once giving up on me and for saving my life. I cannot thank you all enough, especially Kassy, Manj, Vicki, Laura, Tammy, Mike, Fred, Colin. Thank you to my pup Alfi for giving me a reason to get up every morning and making me laugh on days when smiling feels impossible. You're so cute and adorable and I am so lucky to have you. I love you so much.

And my biggest thanks of all has to go to my beautiful girlfriend Rosa; thank you for always being here for me, even when you're 120 miles away. Thank you for your unwavering faith and belief in my ability to truly recover - you gave me that same belief which was a game changer. Thank you for loving me. Thank you for constantly supporting me, inspiring me and motivating me to change. You have helped me see hope for a future that I didn't think could exist. Thank you for introducing me to Brooklyn 99, vegan food, Doughnotts, adventures and a life full of possibilities. Thank you for being honest, kind and for being your true beautiful self. The world is so lucky to have you, as am I and my life is so much brighter with you in it. Thank you for encouraging my dream to publish my poetry; you mean everything to me and I hope you see how much you have influenced me and my writing. I love you with every single bit of me. Always.

# PREFACE

I wrote this book to be able to document my recovery from anorexia nervosa and as an outlet for my emotions. I have always struggled to express my emotions and still find it very difficult to express them in a healthy way. Writing has allowed me to communicate better with my loved ones, carers and has helped me understand myself more. Writing these poems has also helped me realise that things truly can and do get better. I hope reading this book will show you that you are never alone, someone somewhere will understand and you CAN get through the shit life throws at you.

# An ideal body vs an ideal life

I hate my body. Not a day goes by without the feeling of absolute horror and disgust for how I look. This body repulses me. But this body wasn't born to be society's version of beautiful. My body doesn't exist for me to love it (however lovely it would be if I did). My body, my first-time-in-5-years-healthy-body, is for me to LIVE. My healthy body allows me to walk for miles everyday, enjoying the nature around me and practising mindfulness. My body allows me to spend the whole day out with Rosa, from 8am to 10pm and have my primary feeling be of unbelievable happiness rather than exhaustion. This body lets me play with Buddy and run after the ball when he refuses to get it. This body allows my brain to think of things other than food so I can study and ultimately help people. This body allows me to do my volunteering whereas before I was too weak and could barely stand. This body means I am alive and living, not just existing. It actually sort of scares me how I can look like this and still have the same thoughts I had when I was 27kg lighter. But just because I have those thoughts, it doesn't mean I have to act on them. I used to think if I was

always going to have these thoughts I'd rather
be skinny. But skinny, unhealthy, close-to-death
skinny was costing me my life and my LIVING.
I couldn't do what I wanted, what I loved and I
was worrying everyone around me. My mum
would sleep in my room because she was
worried that I wouldn't wake up again. In all
honesty, I think I'll always have my eating
disorder but I will no longer be defined by it. I
will no longer be "the girl with the eating
disorder", "Harri the anorexic". I have fought
too damn hard to let this monster have me, I am
so much more than this awful illness. Don't get
me wrong, I still have days where I cry over a
plate of food or literally over a banana. I still
have days where my exercise urges are out of
control. I still have days when all I want to do is
starve myself and lose all of this weight. I still
have days when I think anorexia brought me
happiness and I think turning back to my old
ways will make me feel better. IT WON'T.
Fighting these thoughts when I looked "ill" was
absolute hell. Fighting these thoughts when I
look "well" is a million, billion times harder.
This battle in my head has been and continues to
be the hardest thing I will ever do, but if it
means I get to LIVE a life I'm PROUD of? You
bet I'm going to do it.

# Little Me

Oh little me, I'm so sorry for the mess you become.
I'm so sorry for the happiness that is taken from you, the light that disappears from your beautiful blue eyes.
I'm so sorry for all of it.
I would give anything to go back to before little me knew what a calorie was.
I would give anything to go back to before little me was conditioned to think that the worst thing someone could be was 'fat' and the best was 'skinny'.
I would give anything to go back to before little me would base her self worth on what number was on that scale.
Before she believed the world was grey, pointless and full of pain.
Before she believed she was worth nothing and should shrink herself accordingly.
Before she believed she had to change to fit in with others, as if being herself wasn't good enough.
Before she believed that life was no longer worth living.
Before she thought she deserved to kill herself.

Before
Before
Before
Give me back that innocence, that simple joy in
just being.
Give me back the happiness of the everyday and
the adventure of the ordinary.
Give me back the pleasure of waking up in the
mornings; I miss wanting to be awake.
Give me the little me back.
Give her back.

# Yet

Yet...
Such an interesting word.
It's like it's inevitable that at some point my self harm will become life threatening.
It's inevitable that at some point my anorexia will cause me to be left with mere hours to live.
It's inevitable that my mental health will become so dangerous that I try to take my own life.
It's inevitable that I will become so sick that I will lose hope with services because I was never 'sick enough'. I'm just not 'sick enough' to deserve their support, therapies, medication, regular appointments, help with money to afford prescriptions. The list is endless.
I will become that sick but I'm not there just 'yet'.
So yes, instead of preventing this assumed inevitable end point of utter self destruction, they'll wait until I get there before they help me. And yet, I could be dead before they come to the conclusion that I'm worthy of their help.
Ah but remember, I'm not dead... yet.

# Abuse disguised as Love

You threw words instead of rocks, I spent all my time watching clocks. I ran far from you but your voice seems to follow me no matter what I do. I thought you were my happiness and my light, but instead you left me crying in pain through the night. You made me hate myself so much, anxious and frightened at every touch. You stole my sparkle and my laugh, you broke and cut me completely in half. I fell for your fools gold, never realising your steel-hard hold. My family tried to tell me but I could not hear, you pushed them away so only you were near. You hurt me without using your hands, your words cut me deeper then you could ever have planned. Love is now a word I cannot use, you've left your mark on me though you see no bruise. Then you left me alone and broken, with so many words left unspoken. You made me feel that death is what I deserve, you made me blind to my own worth. Things would be clearer without your shadow, and maybe I would look forward to a brighter tomorrow. Your darkness swallowed my light, but you never took away my ability to write. So this is my story for whatever it's worth, and let me tell you, it was hell on earth.

# Shrinking

It won't make me happy but being 'bigger' didn't make me happy either. Or so I tell myself. I look back at pictures from that day and the first thing I see is my smile! Not the size of my legs or the width of my hips. I see Harri, with sparkling blue eyes, a smile full of laughter and hope and I see the memories of that day. Not what I ate or how much I weighed that morning, or the morning after that. I remember linking arms with my dad, skipping down the drive knowing I'd finally got my freedom. I had earned it and I was never letting it be taken from me again. I hugged my mum believing I would never spend X amount of months in hospital, away from her again. I was home. Finally, truly home.

I look back now and I feel so much anger and hatred towards myself. I've let anorexia take away my freedom again when I had worked so freaking hard to get it back. I have lost my sparkle, my lust for life that I had finally found. I've lost my hope for a brighter future, my motivation is long gone. I realise now that I'm not as strong as I thought I was. Maybe I'm one of those people who just can't get better - that

Harri in April last year feels like a life time ago, someone so far beyond my reach. The real Harri is gone, and I'm scared, so completely and utterly terrified, that she's gone for good and I've lost my chance to ever get her back.

# Insignificant

I didn't know I could miss someone this much.
Actually I did, but I guess what would be more
accurate would be to say, I didn't know I could
miss someone this much AGAIN. I knew I had
this amount of heart and love within me, I knew
it from the day I met you and I knew it even
more on the day that you left. But I never
thought I would feel this way again, I thought
you were it for me. I saw you as my soulmate,
my future, my landing light. I believed that once
I lost you I had lost the chance of ever being
happy again. It's crazy how wrong you can be
about someone and even more so about yourself.
When I really think about it, I do still miss you
and I think I always will. How one day you were
there and the next you were gone will always
mess with my head, but I think now I care more
about myself than I do about you. Something I
never thought I'd feel.
I still think about you, I still check your profile
to see what's changed, I still ask about you, I
still love you. I guess when it's your first love
that feeling never truly goes away but what I'm
trying to say is that although I wish you well, I
don't wish that you were with me and that's

something I never thought would even cross my mind.

Maybe one day we'll meet and you'll be embarrassed, not sure what to say or how to apologise for how you treated me. I guess I'm not sure what I would say either but I feel better now knowing that whatever you said, whatever you could possibly say? It wouldn't change how I feel about myself, it wouldn't change me now in any way. It would be a comment from someone who I used to know, someone who is now, thankfully, remarkably, completely insignificant.

# That stupid yellow dress

I still have that dress in my closet, the one I
never got to wear, still with all the tags on that I
cannot bear to tear. Saw it in a shop in Portugal
and I couldn't resist, turns out when I didn't turn
up wearing it, I wasn't even missed. That dress
teases me from inside a cupboard that I don't
even look inside, I can't even see it, I can't even
look at it, I make it hide. Am I hiding the dress
or hiding myself? Either way, keeping it isn't
good for my health. Yet I can't give it away, I
can't seem to part with the dress that was meant
to be my freedom, while instead I lay in a
hospital bed, being force fed, beaten. Am I as
broken now as I was then? I know in my heart I
would still go down that same path again. It
hangs there obsolete, like the dreams and
ambitions of 18 year old me, all the things I
thought I would do and who I thought I would
be. A girl left behind because of the evils in her
mind, time just stopped for me. Everyone else
got a future after that night with the dresses,
posting carelessly about their lives and all their
successes. And what have I done in comparison?
What have I achieved? Other than keeping a
dress I'll never even need? Sometimes I wish

that dress would disappear, the memories along with it, the word "prom" resounding in my head with only me left to hear it. I'm so pathetic, still thinking about a dress that still has all the labels on, still reminiscing about a life that's 3 years gone. Maybe one day I'll be able to give it away, maybe one day these words won't cause so much pain just to say. I can't help but think about it at this time of year, with the same wish I had then; that I wasn't really here. Who knew that 3 years on it would still cause me this much distress, just because I never got to wear that stupid yellow dress.

# Healing

14

Whatever the day brings, whatever lies ahead,
whatever your brain tells you, you do deserve to
be fed.
Just be breathing today you have earned your
food, even if you're feeling worthless and
subducd.
Your worth does not decrease because of how
you feel; the therapy and food are essential to
help you heal.

# A different kind of detox

I got rid of those books today, the books that I've been holding on to for years. The books that cause nothing but conflicting comparisons and instant tears. I've held on to them thinking 'I'll need these again, I'll get to rock bottom, do it properly this time'. I've held on to them telling everyone I'm in recovery, telling everyone I'm fine. If I was truly moving on, those books would have gone a year ago but I couldn't bring myself to part with them, feeling, even hoping that I would need them again. They hold a sick sort of sentiment, a trip down memory lane. As if I would want to be that ill again and in that much mental pain. Those books were full of in-depth accounts of something that I've already lived through, as if reading someone else's lowest weight would help me and change my view. The books I read now are fictional tales of things that allow me to escape my own mind, I've read so many and yet so many I am still yet to find. If I read anything to do with eating disorders now, it's how to overcome them, how to recover. Anorexia makes your world so incredibly small when you soon see there's a whole world to discover. Books are now for pleasure again, something to enjoy, not a way to fulfil anorexia's wishes of only to destroy. I've realised that I don't want anorexia anymore, I'm done with the fucked up game she plays. Anorexia hasn't brought me happiness, only tears, hurt and sadness in countless ways. I think I'll always miss anorexia, always just a little bit; but I know now that my eating disorder was a part of me, not I a part of it.

# Some Days

Some days I am Harri and some days I am not.
Some days I focus on what I do have and others
on what I've not.
Some days I complete a list of tasks and other
days I achieve nothing of any significance.
Some days I care too much and some days I
view with complete indifference.
Some days I feel joyful with endless optimism,
others I feel at rock bottom, with nothing left to
live for. Some days opportunity knocks and
other times it's up to me to open the door.
Some days I have goals and plans and some days
I sleep just to pass the time. Some days I tell the
truth but most I lie and say I'm fine.
Some days I can run a mile and others I can't get
out of bed. It all depends on the intensity of the
voices in my head.
Most of the time I am too harsh on myself and I
forget that my best looks different everyday.
Whether it's a mile or just a step, each motion
moves me forward in some small way.

What is it like eating at the table? - a question from my dietician in hospital to help the kitchen staff understand our distress towards food and eating.

Going to the table is stressful and hugely overwhelming. Even just walking from the ward to the dining room is anxiety provoking and a million thoughts race through my mind. I walk past the door to the outside world. I could run if I really tried to. Maybe I could even get away from here?…

In the dining room it's full of people and the table feels so crowded with staff and patients. I feel so self conscious as if everyone is judging me, looking at me, my body, my food, everything. They are judging me for eating and I don't blame them; so am I. The seconds drag while we wait for the food to come out, anxiety rising, thinking of the calories, the fat, the sugar, the GUILT. The food comes out and I blink at the size of the portion. Surely they can't expect me to eat all of that? Picking up my knife and fork takes so much mental effort, having to ignore the incessant argument in my head. The first forkful is the hardest, knowing rationally it is the right thing to do but feeling so intensely how wrong it is too. The torment in my head all the way through, stopping to remind myself to breathe through the forkfuls and the sobs. When it's finally over, that's not the end of the thoughts, the guilt and the tears. I try to breathe, to console myself but then the realisation hits me. That in 2 hours, I have to do it all again.

# Stay

Stay.
Stay for the sunsets.
Stay for the next season of your favourite tv show.
Stay for the takeaway you've got planned next week.
Stay for the people you haven't met yet.
Stay for the doggos that are so fluffy and will always love you unconditionally.
Stay for the late summer nights, laughing with your friends.
Stay for the sequel to your favourite movie.
Stay for that concert next year.
Stay for your favourite dinner that you'll have tomorrow night.
Stay for the flowers.
Stay for Christmas songs and snow.
Stay for the daffodils in spring.
Stay for the dates you'll go on.
Stay for the day that you find your person.
Stay for the chocolate that's left in your cupboard and can't go to waste.
Stay for the thunder storms, cuddled in a blanket, safe.
Stay for the long car journeys to amazing places.

Stay for the books you haven't read yet.
Stay for the music you haven't heard.
Stay for those who love you.
Stay for the Christmas drinks at Costa.
Stay for every smile that is yet to come.
Stay for every reason you have NOT to.
Stay for your reputation of being stubborn as hell.
Stay for the smiles of little babies.
Stay for the walks in the leaves in autumn.
Stay for the fun that hasn't happened yet.
Stay for every single seemingly 'stupid' reason you can think of.
Stay for the person you were, the person you are and the person you have yet to become.
Stay for the hope of a brighter tomorrow.
Just please,
stay.

# "You look well!"

Today I got told I looked "well". Straight away anorexia interpreted that word as "fat", "big", that I've "put on weight", that I'm "huge". But for the first time in a long time, my real response (Harri's response, not anorexia's) was a feeling of pride. I felt happy. I took it as a compliment because recently I have worked so hard, so fucking hard. A bed was ready for me back at Woodbourne and an MHA was being threatened. I had a week to show them all I was serious about doing this at home and I showed them. Not through my weight, not through BMI but through my actions and willingness to work with them as an outpatient. Not to just exist and give excuses in every appointment, not to just float along not "well" but not "critically ill" either. I gave my all to being honest, letting them in, forcing myself to make changes so I wouldn't be forced with a section and a hospital admission. I made myself do at least one challenge everyday. Little by little I worked my way up, little changes day by day that worked out to have a huge impact. I've worked myself out of another admission and proved to everyone, but especially myself, that I can do this. I can make

little changes over time if I'm given support and encouragement rather than force, threats and emotional blackmail. I'm actually dead proud of how far I've come since October, December, even March. Each month brings new challenges and each day feels like hell but if I stop now I'll never know how far I might actually get.
So today, I choose to feel proud of myself. Because who wants to be told they look "ill"? They look "sick", "gaunt", "lifeless" and "deathly"? I used to think I wanted that but I don't. Those things aren't a compliment to me anymore. Looking "well" is. Because looking "well" is people noticing I don't look like death anymore, that I look happier, that I've got light back in my eyes, that I can have a conversation again, that I'm finally getting back to Harri. I've worked hard so when someone says I look "well" now, I'm happy because my progress and determination have paid off. I've worked so hard and for people to see that and say I "look well" shows me that the tears and pain of everyday have been worth it. Worth it because people are finally seeing Harri again, after so many years without her. I refuse to feel ashamed of that.

# Hope

24

Maybe hope is all we'll ever have and need, and
until every last bit of hope is gone there is
always something worth living for.

# Journeys

I know where I'm going and I know where I've
been - I've been down the dark tunnels of gloom
and despair, where nothing lives but an empty
chair. I'm a bad apple fallen far from the tree, all
I've ever wanted in this darkness is to be free.
I've been stuck in the cold of December feeling
nothing but doom, when the rest of the world
has been enjoying the summer of June. I've been
here before and I never meant to be here again
but all I can do now is give it 10 out of 10. No
half-heartedness, no rush, this is the time to do it
tight and come out the other side of this thorny
bush. I've learnt a lot from where I've been and
what I've seen. It's time to let go and see what I
can be; this illness never was and never will be
me. I know where I'm going now even if I'm
unsure how. I know I can get there, I know I can
find my way as long as I dare. I can make it, I
know I can, it will take time but I'm a strong
woman. I am made of fire, fury, strength and
determination, which is how I know that where I
am now isn't my final destination. I want to help
others who've been where I've been and seen
what I've seen. Sometimes on this journey I get
lost, I lose sight of who I am but with the love of

others I remember that I can. My head often tells me lies and leads me to dark places, it's here I get frightened and my heart races. It's here I find that I you look for the light you can often find it, even at the bottom of this dark, dark pit. I know where I'm going now, I'm off on my way, it may not be easy but I'll make it someday. To all those who doubted me, including myself, here's proof that there is hope for me so take me down from the forgotten shelf. I may have scars that show where I've been but they are there to show others that their's too can be seen. There is no blame in where I've been, only hope for the future of what is yet to be seen. I know where I'm going and I know where I've been, the trickiest bit is the time in between. This is the time to show what you can do, no matter what happen just be you. You are enough, worthy and bright; just like at the end of these long dark tunnels, I promise there is light.

# "When you can't look on the bright side, I will sit with you in the dark."

Some of my darkest moments have been brightened by the most unexpected people; people who are struggling immensely and yet find it in their hearts to laugh with me and cry with me when I needed it the most. We have found a unity between us that wasn't our illness, despite that being how we've all happened to meet.
We found unity in friendship, support, guidance and strength.
I have learnt that people can't always find the bright side for you, but they will sit and hold you in the darkness. Together. And I've found that surprisingly, that is so much better.

# I am More

I am so much more than a number on a scale.
I am what I feel and what I think; the thoughts
that flow through my mind like ocean waves.
I am the things that make me happy and the
people that I love.
I am the love I give to other people, with every
piece of my heart, regardless of how broken it
may feel.
I am the stories I tell.
I am the books I read and the hope they bring
when the world seems full of only despair.
I am the music I listen to and the songs I sing at
the top of my lungs.
I am the things that never fail to make me smile,
regardless of how low I'm feeling.
I am everything except those numbers. Those
numbers which do nothing but state my
relationship with gravity.
I am more.

# Monster

This monster is silent to everyone but me, it's
not something anyone can see.
This monster destroys hopes and dreams,
ensuring no one can hear my screams.
This dark, black shadow is sneaky and strong,
it's a trickster, lying that it won't stick around
for very long.
It takes away my freedom and I see that now but
now I want to get rid of it, I don't know how.
This monster started off small but grew in size,
putting obstacles in front of my eyes.
I allow its power, unbeknown to me how truly
powerful it will really be.
This monster can change and look like a friend
when it reality it wants me dead in the end.
This story may sound hopeless and sad but don't
walk away feeling so bad.
This monster is powerful yes that's true, but it's
nowhere as strong as me and you.
This monster is gloomy and gives us a fright but
remember the way to end the darkness is with
our own light.

# Energy Source

The energy we have comes from the sun, the breath in our lungs and the life given from our mum. When did our energy become numbers to ration, to fit in with the crowd, the diets and the fashion. Energy was being able to run and dance; now with so little inside me there's not a chance. Energy was happiness and light in my eyes, now my smile has been taken by anorexia's lies. My energy source should be good food, the sun, my family and hugs from my mum. Love gives us energy with no limit at all, the true nature of anorexia only builds a wall. There is more to me than anorexia can see, it may take my energy but it will not take me.

# Silences

I'm sick of silences round the dinner table as I
push away my food, the shouting and the
arguments putting everyone in a mood. I'm sick
of appointments, weigh ins and ECGs, I miss
being young, carefree and climbing up trees. I'm
sick of medication and terms I don't understand,
I wish you were still here to hold my hand. You
got tired when I got sick, this wasn't the
relationship you chose to pick. Ignoring my
pleas for helping support, you walked out that
door, it seemed, without a second thought. We
used to be so happy and have so much fun, when
I found you I believed my searching was done.
You were mine and I was yours, you gave me
purpose and a cause. When you drifter from me,
I had to find something else to be.
Thinner.
I decided I had to be thinner, but to do this I
couldn't see you or go out for dinner. We fell
further apart but I still saw you as mine, still a
part of my heart. As I became smaller, my
personality did too, so the parts of me you loved
became non-existent for you. Eventually I
stopped speaking so the minutes felt like hours,
the rain persistently pouring, drowning all our

flowers. I was sick of the effects of this illness, you were sick of me being sick, not angry at me but angry at my illness. My illness and I became one, a damaged shell of who I used to be. I thought I did this for you but you actually loved the real me.

# Fear

Conquering fear is the biggest task I now face within the walls of this dark, scary place. There must be a way to other side but it means swimming against the tide. The same tide that has held me back for so long; this fear has taken away my song. To conquer fear would be to conquer this illness but I'm scared that will leave me in a bigger mess. I take a breath and count to ten, get some paper and grab a pen. I write and do and write and do. I find inspiration in music, books and even the news, and despite my lack of faith I take a seat in the church pews. I pray, I hope, I wish, I pray; lord please spare me from another day. Whoever is up there gives me the strength to stand and I look to the person holding my hand. It's me. All along, my support and strength has been me, it's just that I couldn't quite see. I am stronger than I believe and though the fear may not completely leave, I have found a way to conquer it, even just a little bit.

9 789357 446419